www.finishinglinepress.com

The Glass Jar

poems by

Erin Fristad

Finishing Line Press
Georgetown, Kentucky

The Glass Jar

ACKNOWLEDGMENTS

Grateful acknowledgment to the following publications where these poems first
appeared:

"Advice To Female Deckhands." *Stringtown* Issue #8.
"Don't." *Floating Bridge Review #7.*
"Fourteenth Birthday." *Rain Magazine* Spring 2007.
"The Fisherman's Dream" and "Survival Training." *Anchored In Deep Water:
The Fisherpoets Anthology* Edts. Patrick Dixon and Chelsea Stephen.
"What's Left" and "While You Were Sleeping." *Blue Collar Review* Vol. 8
"What This Woman Wants." *Hanging Loose #87.*

Sincere gratitude to all my friends and mentors who've encouraged, cajoled and
demanded this collection; including the three fine artists, Kim Kopp, Marsha
Slomowitz, and Linda Townsend who ushered in the original vision; and Pat
Dixon and Veronica Kessler for an extraordinary amount of generosity and
support with art and life.

Publisher: Leah Maines

Editor: Christen Kincaid

Cover Art: Patrick S. Dixon

Author Photo: Erin Fristad

Cover Design: Elizabeth Maines

Printed in the USA on acid-free paper.
Order online: www.finishinglinepress.com
        also available on amazon.com

Author inquiries and mail orders:
Finishing Line Press
P. O. Box 1626
Georgetown, Kentucky 40324
U. S. A.

Table of Contents

For fifteen years...
and the women in whose wake I followed.

"I realized what we had done; we'd released the lid on the glass jar, the jar of understanding fishermen share. We've all placed things in the jar the outside world can't understand...I understood sitting on that bed in the hotel we have to do this, gather and open the jar before it gets too full and shatters."

"Letter From The Coast"
Alaska Fisherman's Journal: Pilot
House Guide, May 2005

Fourteenth Birthday

The smoke brought a crab boat to our rescue: black steel,
cracks in the storm windows, just back from winter
in the Bering Sea. Unshaven men stood at the rail
peering down at us, one of their heavy tie up lines
landed on our deck, a fire extinguisher stood ready.
Shouts were exchanged. No flames reported.
Smiles formed in their beards. The engineer climbed
down to examine our problem. His thick oil-stained hands
moved with experience. He spit on deck after he talked,
wiped his nose with his sleeve. His advice sounded simple,
they towed us back to the harbor.

Side by side we traveled. I watched lines: taut, slack
taut as our little pleasure boat tried to keep up.
The unshaven men returned, took turns smoking cigarettes,
watching our progress. A woman appeared, dressed like the men
a black wool coat and knee-high rubber boots.
Her hair danced wild around her face. She winked,
gave me a gentle wave. I blushed, looked at my feet.

Before leaving us safe in the harbor, they accepted food
and drinks. They told us of their season, each person
adding details to the story: high winds, shallow waters,
icy decks, plentiful crab and a good price. Sometimes
the speaker would pause, look off over our heads, searching
for the words that could make us understand
living on the ocean, through the season of darkness,
on the rise and fall of thirty-foot waves. I surveyed the boat:
contents of the window sills, slow turn of the radar, dents
along the hull, orange and yellow raingear hanging
from the back of the house. The woman caught me staring,
motioned me closer, offered her hand from over the rail.

Untying

Bulging backpacks
crowd bunks.
A pile of rubber boots
fills the corner.
Lettuce, milk,
a melting block of ice—
the last bag of groceries
sits on the galley table.
Everyone moves
like they've had too much coffee,
repeatedly running into each other,
not yet adjusted
to this small world.

We stash the crab pot,
barbecue,
outboard motor.
Someone is looking
for the foot pump
to the inflatable skiff.
We keep busy
while the last guy
says good-bye
to his girlfriend.
They'll marry in the fall.

The lines hit the dock
with a thud.
They're wet as we pull them
back through hawseholes
marking the beginning
of three months of wet hands.
Forward, reverse, forward, reverse—

our legs absorb the boat's motion
as it works away from the dock.

Our chatter ends.
We coil lines,
tie up buoy bags,
tighten down hatch covers.

Each one of us will pause
standing near the rail,
eyes closed, the salt air
tingling our faces.
We'll listen
to the slowing of our pulses,
our bodies becoming lighter,
the noise of our lives
growing distant
behind us.

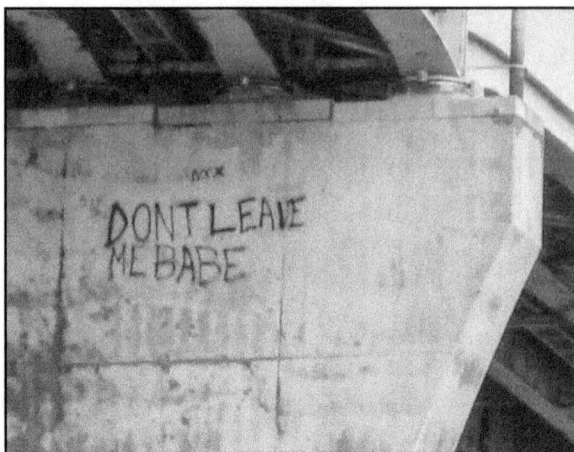

Don't

None of us knew who wrote it or remembered when it first appeared. It was part of the landscape, but we looked at it in awe every time we passed under the Fred Zharoff Bridge. It meant different things depending if you were coming or going from the fishing grounds, if you'd made money or not. On sunny afternoons without raingear, without our hoods on, when it warm enough to look up, we pondered out loud: who? And more importantly; did it work? Often a new guy, trying to impress us, would say he knew the guy whose girlfriend did it. The other new guy would cut him off, "No, man it was the dude's wife and he died before he ever saw it."

"You're both wrong," I'd say. "It was a crewmember I worked with in the eighties. I remember the night he did it. The crab season ran long that year. We were making money, but all the crab were out west in Dutch and we only came to town once: to pick up more pots. We had 24 hours to see our wives and kids.

They made love; actually, they probably fucked like starved animals the way we all did our first night back. Then they fell asleep curled in a ball and he dreamed of eating bacon with his kids in the morning. The phone woke him, 'Boat leaves in an hour, there's a front moving in.' She went ballistic. He hadn't even seen the kids. She told him if he left, she would too, head to her sister's in Phoenix. She'd have the divorce papers filed before the season was over.

It was snowing hard when I pulled up and she was chasing him down the front walk punching his hunched-over back with her little pink fists. She was barefoot, her silk robe falling open. I remember thinking *where do you get a robe like that in Kodiak?* She threw a garbage can lid at my truck as we pulled away. He was silent but I could see the tears running down his face in the light from oncoming cars. He pulled out a flask and took a long pull. I never told him but when I looked back his two kids had come outside, the little was one trying to catch snowflakes in her mouth.

We arrived at the boat and he disappeared. Skipper was anxious to leave. I stalled by saying the main needed an oil change. I heard the guys screaming on deck and thought he'd fallen overboard. I ran topside and realized they were cheering. There he was hanging from the bridge, he'd lowered himself down using a tie-up line. He had paint we used to mark buoys."

This shuts the new guys up. They don't want to know what happened next. They don't want to know if it's true.

First Responder

It's less glamorous than you would think. Despite the training, the clearing of Annie's airway, the discharging of fire extinguishers, practice grounding the helo cable, stabilizing of necks and spines: most injuries at sea don't require an airlift—most don't even justify a trip to town. The coast guard class doesn't prepare you for a 19-year-old hit in the face with a buoy stick. There's no film showing you how to butterfly the three-inch gash with cheap bandages from Fred Meyer. It doesn't provide you with reassuring phrases like, "This scar will make a good story to tell your girlfriends." It doesn't tell you the 19-year-old won't care because he's never imagined living long enough to regret a scar. The film doesn't include the part where he pulls out his cell phone, shows you a photograph of a "real head wound," his scalp peeled back, his brain pink and wet. The photo was taken the night he drove his stepmom's Fiat into a telephone pole. "Of course I was drunk," he'll boast "sober fucks don't survive an accident like that." Then he'll tell you the "funny part": his father was first to the scene and discovering him alive, beat the shit out of him. It was his father's patrol that night, his stretch of winding highway, in the photo you'll see the blue light of his squad car.

While You Were Sleeping

To witness mindfully is to grieve for what has been lost.
Freeman House

By August 15th, everyone knows the fish
aren't coming. Your skipper buys
a pickup truck, starts drinking
and driving. The crew joins him.
You wear large hats, put the dogs in between you,
drive to the neighboring fishing village. You make up
some silly reason for this ritual, perhaps luck,
but you all know it's better
than staring at an empty ocean.
At the first mile marker, you snap
your bottle caps out the window,
raise your beers in a symbolic toast
and look straight ahead.
You know it's the end, the first end.
You joke about working at McDonalds
but lay awake at night staring out the fo'c'sle
hatch thinking of who you might call
for a construction job over the winter
or maybe another fishery. You calculate
how much money you'd make in three months of trawling,
then imagine leaving Seattle the day after Christmas,
New Year's Eve puking out the wheelhouse window
somewhere in of the Gulf of Alaska encased
in darkness. You think about crossing
icy decks and balancing on your knees to bleed fish.
This image makes you sick to your stomach
turning on your side you think:
maybe the fish will hit tomorrow.
Trying to fall asleep you imagine
telling this story five years from now:
a late run of Sockeye, a jump in the price
of Chums, your end of the season dinner
filled with good wine and laughter.

Your optimism swells enough
to let you sleep. What you can't imagine
is five years from now
you'll be painting yachts and sailboats
in a dusty boatyard in the lower forty-eight.
You don't know this yet, you're still sleeping
to the sound of a refrigeration system chilling water
for fish you won't catch. What you don't know
is that the fish will come back, next season,
but no one will want them. You still believe
a low return will bring up the price
next year, like in high school economics—
it will all balance out in the end.
But you can't imagine the end.
An eight hour work day, a paycheck every two-weeks,
shorts, flip-flops, sitting in traffic watching the heat
rise from blacktop. You'll be standing
around a barbecue, someone will joke
about a town full of fishing refugees. You'll notice
the man next to you leaning slightly forward,
his feet too far apart, braced for the swell.
You can't imagine sitting at a desk
in August, reading books about salmon,
trying to learn the scientific terms
for what they do. You'll catch yourself
studying the pictures, trying to name the river,
trying to find a rock you once rested on.
You'll stare so long you'll start to smell
the rotting carcasses. But for now,
I watch you sleeping.
In another hour, you'll wake
and pull anchor.

What's Left

The voice on the phone says flatly,
"We've been forced to lay off some boats."
A long pause implies he's one of them.
His response equally flat. He fantasizes
calling them bastards, ranting about pathetic
marketing, price fixing, how unfair it feels
being forced out by huge steel boats that fish three
or four fisheries, with three or four hired
skippers. But the voice on the phone
is familiar, a man he met when
he was eighteen walking the docks
looking for his first fishing job.
This same man called to congratulate
him when he bought his own boat.
This is the man who arranged his cannery loan. Truth is
they're both sorry, and that's what they say,
and silence and they hang up.
What's left of a fisherman laughs
at the words "laying off boats."
"You're laying off people you bastards"
finally escapes between a shout
and a whisper. A noise brings him back,
his four year old daughter pushes the door
open, she's giggles, bounces, points.
She wants him to see their golden
retriever wearing a sweatshirt, struggling,
wagging his tail, trying to please her. Now he's a father,
petting his dog, tickling his daughter, directing
them back out into the yard. What if I tell you
it's not that bad for this man? What if his boat is paid for,
his wife is a teacher, they have health insurance,
they own their cars? A young couple from Seattle

has phoned twice, desperate to buy
a classic wood boat, turn the fishhold
into state rooms. What if I tell you
he has a teaching certificate
he'll find work, maybe get his captain's license
run a small tour boat in the summer. But I can't let go
of the phone call, the one where he found out
the sale was final. I can't forget that same afternoon
when he drove to the harbor, sat in his truck staring
at his new boat in the slip. He walked down the dock
alone, climbed on board. I can smell it, wet wood
diesel. There he is lighting the stove
warming his hands over the flame.

The Year the Sockeye Returned

The western stock of the Steller's sea lion has been in continuous decline since the 1970s. The extent of this decline led the National Marine Fisheries Service to list the Steller's sea lion as threatened range-wide under the Endangered Species Act in April of 1990.
National Marine Mammal Laboratory

The salmon fishermen of Alaska should be listed under the Endangered Species Act.
Glenn Reed, Executive Director Pacific Seafood Processors Association.

It was the busiest ever, for species on and off the boat.
Sea lions chewed our net, bit fish in half, skipper's raised fist cursed them
away.
A deckhand advised: "A shot to the head so the body won't float."

A rifle appeared, skipper charged shouting: "The fish are mine, don't goad
me on." Hungry and stubborn: fishermen and sea lions' shared traits.
We were the busiest ever, predators with and without a boat.

The sea lions stayed. Skipper sure they were gloating
screamed: "Bastards! They'll cut into our day's pay."
A deckhand advised: "A shot to the head so the body won't float."

They continued to feast and a terrible roar escaped skipper's throat.
The crew ducked low, the barrel smoked, sea lions dived to get away.
We were the busiest ever, predators with and without a boat.

The shot was fired, the sea's swell made the target remote.
Skipper held a piercing stare, confident his aim would never stray.
A deckhand prayed: a shot to the head so the body won't float.

The sea lion lived, and I knew this should never be wrote.
It's a code among fishermen I've chose to betray.
We were the busiest ever, predators on and off the boat.
The skipper jested: "a shot to her head so the body won't float."

Advice to Female Deckhands

You will be the cook.
In addition to wheel watches, working
on deck, unloading fish, fueling up,
filling fresh water, mending nets,
grocery shopping whenever you come to town,
you will also prepare three meals a day
and two hearty snacks to go with coffee.
You must keep the kettle on the stove full
and the juice jug and two gallons of milk in the fridge.

You will learn to slice vegetables, prepare a marinade,
cook pasta and fillet a salmon
in twenty minute intervals
while the net is out. You will learn
to ignore the other crew members sitting
at the galley table reading. You must know
how to create a corral in rough weather,
so pots of soup don't end up dripping
down the firewall behind the stove. You will need
bungie cords to keep the cast iron skillet from sliding.
These cords melt if they touch the stovetop.
Keep a squeeze container of Aloe Vera gel
under the galley sink for the burns
on your hands and forearms.

The stove will blow out on windy days
when you're exhausted,
your skin stinging with jellyfish.
The crew will say they're not hungry on these days
but when you slide behind the Cape, it will be flat
calm and all of you will be starving.
Before relighting the stove
determine how much diesel has built up.
If it's more than an inch deep,

turn off the fuel source
by flipping a breaker in the engine room.
You don't have time for ear protection. Get down there
and back before someone hollers for you on deck.
Passing the engine, watch the straps on your raingear,
your ponytail, where you put your hands.

When cooking, remember all odors from the galley
drift directly into the wheelhouse. Fish sauce
smells like dirty tennis shoes. Once she smells this,
your skipper's daughter will refuse to eat anything
she suspects has fish sauce. As a woman and cook
you will be expected to have a special bond
with the skipper's daughter
and you will. Have art supplies in a shoebox in the galley,
a drawing tablet under a cushion, collect starfish,
Decorator crab, and Spiny Lump Suckers in a deck bucket.
Teach her what you know can kill her. When she cries
put your arm around her, kiss her
on the top of the head and let her cry.
Allow her to use your cell phone to call friends
in exchange for making salads, pots of coffee,
washing lunch dishes, carrying groceries to the boat.
Develop sign language for communicating
when she stands in the galley door
peering out at you on deck.

This isn't what I intended.
I set out to give you advice for taking care
of yourself, now it's about taking care of a girl
you're related to by circumstance.
This is exactly what will happen.
You'll notice a hum
more penetrating than the engine.

The Fisherman's Dream

I should have known I was dreaming because I carefully backed down the wheelhouse ladder, like children are taught, watching my feet, like greenhorns do. I never do that. I go up and down that ladder 50 times a day and I always face forward coming down. I like to see what I'm walking into. I like to know if the crew is reading at the galley table when there's work to do. But this time, I carefully make my way to the bottom and turnaround.

There she is at the galley sink. She's cleaning up from dinner. She's busy and doesn't acknowledge me. I watch her bend down to get something from under the sink and her red thong underwear show over the top of her Carhartts. This never fails to turn me on. I don't know who is driving the boat at this point and I don't care. I walk over, put my arm around her waist and kiss her neck from behind. She giggles pushes me away with her elbow but in the same motion she turns and kisses me. God this girl can kiss. She engulfs me like she has the mouth of a Ling Cod. I know that shouldn't be sexy but it is, she's full on, she doesn't hold back, she doesn't portion out her affection she devours me whole. Now she's facing me, kissing me, both her hands holding my head pulling me closer, closer into her lips, into her love. I hold her waist, it seems small under my fisherman's hands, but this girl is strong as an ox. And fast. She moves across deck like lightening. I never tell her what to do. It's done before I think of it. The guys don't even try to keep up. She's of the ocean, she's got generations of fisherman's blood pumping through her veins. Thinking this I kiss her harder, I plunge deeper. The momentum pushes her back onto the galley table. I'm on top of her, I want her now; I want her on the galley table. Then the engine slows, she pushes me off, "We're at the tender, time to unload." She's gone. I'm so hard I can barely walk. She's out on deck pulling up her rainpants. She grabs the socket wrench and starts unbolting the hatch cover. I watch in awe and disappointment. She catches me watching and winks. She knows I want her. She knows I can't resist her Ling Cod lips. I image her red thong underwear rubbing against the inside of her rainpants.

She brushes up against me when she turns the hydraulics on, but she's not flirting with me now. She's getting ready to lift the hatch cover off the fishhold. She directs me to work the controls. Her lips are pursed. She's looking up, lining up the boom with the center of the hatch cover, giving me direction with her fingers. She hooks it up, gives me the motion to lift, guides it across the deck, gives me the motion to set it down.

This is where it gets scary and I don't know why I can't wake myself up. They say you should be able to wake yourself up from a nightmare, but I can't. I'm looking up from the fishhold. I'm in there with the fish. I'm watching the beautiful girl move across deck and then I see myself step out from the controls and look down at me in the fishhold, but the me looking down isn't me. It's my wife. She looks right at me. She has the mouth of a Wolf Eel. I gasp. I dive to get away. But I can't breath. I have to come back up to the surface. I see them both together, my wife and my girlfriend standing at the edge of the fishhold looking down at me.

It gets worse. I realize they don't see me, they don't recognize me, I'm a fish. I'm just another caught fish swimming around in the hold waiting to die. I don't dive. I linger at the surface watching my wife and my girlfriend. My girlfriend's Ling Cod lips rise at the corners in a smile, my wife laughs, tosses her head back revealing the sharp edges of her hideous Wolf Eel teeth. Then she leans over and kisses my girlfriend. She kisses her hard and my girlfriend kisses back. I can't take this betrayal. I leap from the hold and land on deck at their feet. My wife laughs, "nice try buddy but you've been caught" and she pushes me back into the hold with her foot.

Survival Training

The good news is that he is a drunk and doesn't remember what he did. I'm expected to take solace in this: a good man prone to excess and blackouts. He's repeatedly described as harmless, and an excellent skiff driver. I tell his supporters he's the most graceful drunk I've ever seen, leaping rail to rail wearing only his whitey-tighties, arms spread like wings so he lands gently on deck. So graceful it appears intentional, as though not to wake his sleeping crewmates. But maybe he is harmless. My dog didn't seem too upset by his masturbating in the galley. She focused on protecting her food dish just in case he had a fondness for kibble. This is the joke I adopt in light of my crewmates growing irritated with me, telling me, "let it go, it was no big deal, there are guys far worse than Dave floating around out here." I wear my little joke like a survival suit. It keeps me afloat three months. Then Rufus stops by. I didn't make up that name and yes, he was born in West Virginia, but he came to the fishing fleet via Wyoming where he worked twenty years as a prison guard. He doesn't bother sitting down, just stands in the galley door and slowly shakes his head as he listens, "God damn it girl, ya shoulda' beat him with a baseball bat."

Final Day of the Season

The net is out. We stand on the back deck with arms slack at our sides. We don't bother taking off raingear, drinking coffee, or washing down the deck. We don't care if we stand in the bite of the towline. Our remaining energy is used to argue, like siblings in the back seat of the family station wagon returning from a vacation where we've all suffered food poisoning and sunburns. We are deflated human air mattresses with too many leaks to patch. Tall Gary says that's a stupid metaphor because an air mattress would have been horizontal in the last three months. We fantasize about how today will end and argue about that too. I imagine a value on a pipeline being cranked closed, the stream of salmon halted, an old hunch-backed man pulling a plug and draining the ocean. The boat will gently rest on the bottom, with only a slight list, and we'll simply jump the rail and walk to town. Short Gary shakes his head in dismay, "Under that water it's 25 miles of steep, muddy canyons. It'll take you a week to reach Ketchikan. Me, I have a history of mental illness and a Jesus complex. I'm walking on water straight to the airport, not a speck of mud on me. I'm buying a ticket out of Alaska; consuming numerous drinks in the bar; and for your information, the plane will be full of hookers who work pro bono."

Wishes for Fishermen

It'll be poetry all day.
3 am and you'll prepare
my coffee, butter my toast,
boot up the computers,
pull out the thesaurus,
rhyming dictionary
and *Handbook of Poetic Forms.*

By dawn we'll have completed
our warm up exercise:
a list of ten fears
and a secret you've never told anyone.
That might work in a sestina,
you have an hour to try.
We'll read our poems out loud.
No wait, we'll trade poems
listen to our words coming
from someone else's mouth.

For lunch, prepare something we can eat
while writing. Remember: I only eat fish,
one guy is allergic to nuts,
one can't eat mayonnaise.
But it shouldn't be too much trouble
to fix him something on the side, should it?
I'll tell you I don't eat dessert
then empty every cabinet in the galley
looking for cookies. You'll need to clean up
quickly, it's dangerous to write in a mess.

Next exercise: a letter poem
addressed to the person
who made you grow up
too fast. Tell him

you should have been left alone
to stomp through creek water,
pants soaked to the thighs,
left to pursue salmon
hiding in pools
under fallen trees.
Tell him you would have stood
perfectly still
watching one salmon
make its way back into the current,
its body a giant muscle bending
with unconscious determination.

"Unconscious determination?"
I'll underline this on your rough draft,
scribble in the margin,
"too abstract, can you be more concise?"
Show me what drives the salmon,
show me the flavor and smell of fresh water,
show me what the logical mind doesn't know,
show me how the salmon will die another mile upstream.
Show me how we all go on
unable to recognize our final landscape.

Eventually, there will be a break in the poetry.
You'll prepare dinner.
Someone passing through the galley
will pick up one of your books on fishing,
flip through it, read two lines, toss it down
and declare: "I've never really
understood this stuff."

After you've cleared away the dishes
we'll gather and read our best lines out loud.
Repeating them over and over to each other
delighted with the punch of a spondee,
the seduction of slant rhyme.
You'll wander off. At first, we'll not notice
as you lower your monofilament line
overboard, the perfect jigging rhythm
of your wrist, your eye on the current, your ears
perked for a jumper. You'll reel in
the flasher just below the surface
and let it sink again. This motion
will set you adrift
far away from this boat
of all poetry. One of us will stand
in the galley door watching, thinking
yours is a romantic pursuit.

Navigating in the Fog

I'm on the wheel
southbound at Bella Bella
beginning the tight squeeze into Lama Pass.
It's daylight, but that's irrelevant
fog so thick I can't see
the anchor chalk.

I straddle the old Furuno radar
rest my forehead on the viewer
watch the green sweep,
hear the voice of my first skipper:
don't look out the window
trust only the radar.
I adjust the range wanting
to know what's ahead
quarter mile to half mile:
all I get is a green indiscernible mass.
Back to quarter mile
the outline of a familiar island.
My first skipper returns:
Hold your course.

The smell of fresh coffee
arrives from the galley,
buoyant voices fill
our floating, wooden world.
I stretch my neck, exhale,
return to the radar, my forehead
sticking to the rubber
holding me there, the sound
of its old motor mesmerizing
like the pump of a fish tank,
or a lover breathing in the dark.

I let it cradle me
thinking those old timers
designed a smart radar.
They knew every mariner
is eager to be held
even a brief moment
as though Calypso herself
took my head in her hands.
Those old timers knew
what it would take to keep us
from fighting ourselves;
knew the danger of trying
to see in the fog
how our eyes play tricks on us
land appearing too close
or not at all.

The marine radio breaks the silence:
"Tug and tow northbound Bella Bella."
My heart rate increases, mouth goes dry
I drop the wheelhouse window
hear the low roar of an engine not ours:
Don't look out, don't look out.
I return to the radar
watch the familiar island
peel into two as the tug pulls away.
I hear their bow wake approaching
pray their cable tight, tow short.
I lean harder into the radar:
Hold your course, this is the tight spot,
don't overcorrect.

Their stern wakes slaps our hull
moving us like an old, wooden, rocking horse.
Still leaning into the radar
I correct to port as the passage widens
my thoughts return to the smell of coffee,
blessing our floating, wooden world.
I'm telling you this story because navigating
is another word for love. Your heart
is your radar and you should never
trust your eyes.

Praise This Dark and Windy Morning

far from the fishing grounds,
far from automated voices
dispatching marine weather,
far from the alarm on the sounder,
far from chatter in the rigging.

Praise not balancing on one foot
in the galley doorway struggling
rainpants over xtra-tuffs. Praise
not pulling the anchor, not wrestling
cable onto the drum, rain not pelting
my hunched figure. Praise wind
not forcing me to squint.
Praise my ball cap not blowing off.

Praise not wearing a ball cap.

Praise not peeking out around
Cape Constantine,
Cape Ulitka,
Cape Addington,
Cape Flattery,
Cape Disappointment.

Praise not deciding
whether or not
to fish.

Praise the gentle beep
of an alarm clock and not
the explosive roar of a Jimmy.

Praise my desk, my computer,
my electric heater warming my feet.
Praise the sound of two dogs snoring,
and the optimistic crackle
in the wood stove.

Praise drinking coffee without
the taste of rainwater
or saltwater. Praise my coffee cup
motionless. Praise the gas stove
that boiled the water to make my coffee
and did not suffocate
in a back draft through a galley door.

Praise the 59-inch-width
of my queen-sized bed.
Praise sleeping naked
on flannel sheets.
Praise stretching out my legs
without hitting the bulkhead.
Praise not rolling over
onto my flashlight,
Sibley's Guide to Birds,
seven books of poetry,
the novel I've started
twenty times.

Praise every crewmate
with a sleeping disorder that involves:
gasping for breath,
choking,
screaming,
shouting,
or farting poisonous gas.
Praise the distance between us.

Praise not dressing in my bunk,
a dark fo'c'sle, or loud engine room.
Praise the engineer not fishing
my thong underwear from the bilge.
Praise he has not left them for display
on the galley table.

Praise every storm we weathered.
Praise every game of Scrabble,
Cribbage, Gin Rummy. Praise
vodka in plastic bottles. Praise
weird deckhands, mean skippers,
bear stories and angry ex-wives
who gave us something to talk about.

Praise every anchor dropped
because of a dead engine, tide rip,
reef, rock pile. Praise
your galvanized weight,
shape of your flukes,
strength of your cable.
Praise every anchor that held
allowing us to sleep.

Praise every anchor that holds right now,
far from the safety of this poem.
I hear the wind pulling your load
against you, hold fast
so those aboard will learn to praise
what will soon be gone.

What This Woman Wants

I want to walk like I'm the only
woman on earth and I can have my pick.
Kim Addonizio

Keep your red dress and spiky
bad girl shoes. Give me a steel boat
with water-tight doors,
double-paned windows,
an anchor that'll hold
in an eighty-knot blow. Better yet,
make me this boat. Paint my hull black
so when I pull into the harbor at night,
people strain to see the source of my hum.
Don't bother with tie-up lines;
this boat rises from the water,
levitates, cruises the streets.
This boat doesn't sleep.

My radar turns, catches the eye
of a boy smoking pot
in front of a television
while his parents argue upstairs.
He hoists himself on board,
tosses his coat in an empty bunk.
A girl counts the days on her calendar,
counts again, hopes for blood,
hopes her boyfriend won't arrive drunk
outside her window. My running lights
move across her bedroom wall. She lands
on my back deck. The old man wakes,
thinking of grandchildren
tired of his stories, his daughter cringing
from the whiskey on his breath—
he wishes his memory would fail.
Out the window, he notices stars
reflected on my black steel.
The last bar closes, the bartender walks,

her ex-boyfriend waits, she shakes
her purse searching for keys.
My bow nudges this scene to a close.
He picks gravel from his palms. The others
lift her aboard.

By dawn, my deck is crowded.
There is a long splash as my hull
dips back into the harbor. We slip out
around the breakwater,
set course into the ocean swell.
In my galley, eggs break
into a mixing bowl, olive oil
heats on cast iron,
someone slices bread for toast.

Afterward

It Calls Me Back

Arrives every spring
like a head cold,
best I can do is treat the symptoms
drive slowly southbound
over The Ballard Bridge,
strain to see Fishermen's Terminal
name boats, look for a familiar
silhouette moving across deck.
I'll call my favorite skippers, in case
someone's wife put her foot down
or being away from a giggling three-year-old
just wasn't worth it. I call in case I can leave
all the obligations that settled in
staying in one place too long. I even bought
a new pair of Extra Tuffs. Pulled my sea bag down
from the top shelf in the hall closest
dug out the Atlas gloves, blue elf-feet booties,
my black, wool halibut jacket.

The Extra Tuffs haven't gone fishing,
but I packed them to Homer, wore them
in the water-taxi to Tutka Bay, wore them
to read poetry on a helicopter landing pad
turned fine dining experience where bankers,
business owners, the Director
of the Chamber of Commerce
paired my words with muscles, salmon,
halibut, the fishing boats they see
from a distance. Now those Extra Tuffs
wait in the barn, where I slip them
on and off twice daily
to clean stalls and feed horses.

The Swede still visits me
a couple nights a month. Striding
into my dreams convinced he's the skipper

of everything. He told me he fell in love with me
the first time I set the break on the trawl winch,
fell harder watching me leverage
a guide stick to wind cable
onto the drum. Swore he'd leave his wife
before the engineer called bullshit
on our risky behavior, hired Chuck to weld up
a set of fairleads, disappearing
the guide sticks forever.
It's an odd phenomenon how
having a woman on deck
suddenly makes normal-dangerous
appear stupid-dangerous.
Or how that same woman can get you
to look up, watch a cloud
of herring scales glistening
under deck lights, how you'll laugh
in a strange gratitude as they cover
your raingear like sequin.

I miss our gimbaled reality,
falling asleep to the sound
of humpbacks breathing,
Stellar Sea Lions arguing,
generators chilling water.
I miss the motion of rolling a cigarette,
the slow numbing of Bushmills.
I miss honesty that reaches
to the edge of sodium lights
on a December night. Confessions
of infidelities, police raids, buried guns,
one guy born in prison,
all of them with children
they'd do anything for—
except leave this: weeks and months gone
to where even the lies are true.

I can feel it now, typing these words
desire knocking in my chest
to be awake at the edge of uncertainty,
possibility, the constant allure
of what's next. My addictions are all lined up
holding hands, calling me back, daring me to see
the season's first pot clear the rail,
daring me to hear the bear trap hit the deck,
daring me to watch the cod-end break the surface
a writhing sea monster porpoising in our wake.

Erin Fristad is of the Northwest: she is the spawn of loggers, miners and commercial fishermen. She survived 15 years as a deckhand on a wide array of vessels and adventures. She chased herring near Togiak, crab off the Columbia River, salmon more places than she can remember; and for five years pursued fish in the name of science. Towards the end of her fishing era, she returned to graduate school to earn her MFA in Creative Writing from Goddard College.

Erin is a founding member of a community of writers connected by commercial fishing and the maritime industry. She is a regular reader at their annual festival, The Fisher Poets Gathering, which has been covered by The *New York Times*, *Smithsonian Magazine* and in an award-winning documentary film, FISHER POETS.

Erin's work has appeared in journals and anthologies including *Rosebud, americas review, The Blue Collar Review, Hanging Loose, The Seattle Review, Floating Bridge Review, Working the Woods, Working the Sea: An Anthology of Northwest Writing, New Poets of the American West, Raising Lilly Ledbetter: Women Poets Occupy The Workspace* and *Hooked! True Stories of Death, Obsession and Love From Alaska's Commercial Fishing Men and Women.*

Erin currently lives in Washington State where she works as a writer, educator, facilitator...and itinerant farmhand. You can learn more at www.erinfristad.com.